03/30/20

Kyle,
Thank you for
supporting me.

♡ Hails

Hailey Beard

Welcome to the/our
process.

The Society Of Process

Cover design by Hailey Paige Beard
Interior illustrations by Hailey Paige Beard

Independently published through Amazon KDP
ISBN: 979-8-61-907366-9

Hailey Paige Beard / Hailey Paige

West Palm Beach, FL

To all my family, friends and strangers for being a part of this process. I honor you and the Ultimate Healer for the space you've held with me. I also want to celebrate and say many thanks to Michal, Taylor and Macy for all walking me through this dream becoming a reality. I couldn't have done it without you.

The Society Of Process

Written & Illustrated
by Hailey Paige

Contents

This book is for all the hearts that are fearful, resilient, brave, fickle, bleeding, weak, whole and more.

Our hearts are in process as we learn how to heal, grow and move throughout this life of ours. Please allow this book to be a space for you to look at your own story and allow your heart to just be, to feel and heal. In this life we often move too quickly, wanting to skip the process, yet this is where we are refined. So let's become aware of the space in our hearts and honor the healing journey.

A dear friend of mine, Monika, wrote this poem and I believe it eloquently invites us into this book together,

Resilient heart / fickle heart
You're not stronger for staying
Nor weaker for going

Brave heart / fearful heart
You're not wrong for trying
Nor bad for retreating

Whole heart / bleeding heart
You are as beautiful in fragments
As you were at first

I do love you when you're tender,
Dear heart
I wanted to say, it's okay.

Living in the Downpour

Oh brave girl,

You are far more fearless than I
Chaos is only known when it is adored by the wild and not the weak
You are made for far more beautiful conditions
While you stand in the monsoon of flawed perceptions
Remember that you are valiant
You are known
And if not for life's mess
Would you truly be living?

No Ordinary Lens

I am not ordinary in the slightest
Brought on many endeavours
Used and cherished
Capturing moments forever

My eyes
Snap what is to be remembered
Those warm summer nights
Or pure ones in December

Passed down through the years
With many beholders
From Papa to Jimmy
With different exposures

For I am no ordinary lens
Experiences that cannot be recreated
I seize with hope
For our hearts to be illustrated

The Inner Me

My inner child is trapped
Imprisoned
Disappointed
Isolated
They will leave
Always
As I interact with my adult world,
And the crippling lack of stable bonds
How can I let myself be loved or understood
I long to make up for this stolen childhood
Back to prove myself worthy of the love that I hope others feel
for me
The thing is
They will never live up to the unrealistic expectations of my
juvenile heart

God invade the deep wounds that remain
Air them out completely
Restore without blemish
Allow me to feel your love, to love, and to let love

Consuming

As often as the clock hand ticks
And the morning calls the sun
Thoughts of you consume me

Your heart is so foreign to me
Yet your eyes so kind
And so familiar

I find myself scanning the crowd, hoping to see your face
Longing to feel your touch
To give these fluttering flies life
Because thoughts of you consume me

I seem to claim destiny in moments where our locations collide
And my heart stops to take a breath when I overhear your favorites,
because our favorites are friends
And I want to scream to the world of our harmony

I crave the taste of your sweet disposition
And to know the thumping of your temperament
Though all of you has no idea how you exhaust my frame
Because the depth of our accord is hollow

 But maybe today,
Today I'll muster the courage
Or better yet, maybe you will
And in fact, I hope you do
Because thoughts of you are consuming

Summertime Heroin

I have been a slave this eternal summer
Held captive to the sunny drug of Florida flowers
Unable to remember the seasonal droughts that suck the life dry

I have been living amongst the winter-absent palm trees
This never-ending summer however is now changing course
For the sun seems to be becoming dimmer by day
Over the horizon is the decay
As if I am driving into the thickness of a suffocating winter

Life has no favorites
For it grows and flourishes
Then falls, decomposing to dust

Oh please, sun, don't leave me
I was just getting used to what it felt like to stay warm
I'm fearful of a winter without you
Who will keep me company
The summertime heroin in my root system strong
I already feel the detox and thirst for you
When will your companion spring be due to town
I don't know how long I can hold off this addiction

Jellies

I invade your world for my own enjoyment
Your neighborhood, though, I hope to avoid
The shiny transparency of you is so attractive
Yet your touch
Leaves me wounded

Your venomous arms that embrace me
Jolting me with anxiety and pain
While your abyss is uncharted
Because the nature of you, inconsistent

Blindly I enter again and again
To seek refuge from my own space
The location of you forever unknown
And you attack without any warning
I have no worries until it's too late

However, the risk of your sting is
Still not enough to keep me away

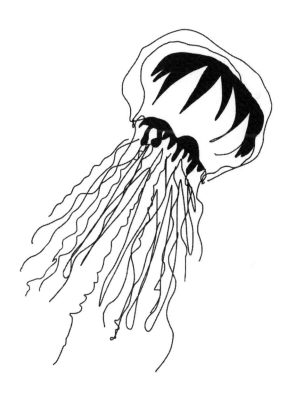

Dear Nonexistent

An open letter to our nonexistent relationship
I feel in love with you in secret
And now I can't breathe around you
I tell my mind that we are together
The way you look at me and smile
Tell me I look beautiful
You don't do that to any of the other girls
So you must love me right?

Blended

Blended
Offended
Persecuted
Barely Defended

Blacks milled
Blood spilled
Hearts chilled
While men are being killed

Where does this stop
Does it start with the cops
Are they the ones on top
This too messy to mop

Separate but equal
Nothing seems peaceful
Are the accusations legal
This battle's medieval

The law has been amended
Now bonds need to be mended
Not to forget what was that men did
Blended hearts need be recommended

To The Palm Trees

The question was painless
Exchange clear
So easily I traded the oaks for the palms
The crisp autumn air for a never ending summer breeze
Brisk wind like a current on my arm for the warmth of water
between my toes
The flexibility of seasons for a consistent affection
Deceased leaves that crunch under my feet like chips
 For the pool of sand in every pair of shoes I own
Effortlessly, I swapped the emerald corn pastures for a
renaissance island city
Spirits High
This isle became my safe haven
A neighborhood I grew so fond of
And companions who became my refuge
Coffee shops that became my asylums
Enough espresso and pastries that filled my soul
This retreat to the coconut trees became my sanctuary
So godspeed, Mr.Oak
To the palm forest I flee

Waiting

There is so much I want to share with you
Moments of connection where our eyes synced
As a grin appeared on your face
And my heart began to beat more intensely
And it's like my heart is screaming to grab your hand
Your face
Anything to feel you
I thought for sure you would have to finally bend
But again
You haven't
I wait
Holding my breath
Again
And I've gotten pretty good at it now
In your presence
Only coming up for air when I absolutely am in need
Quite ironically I don't know if you are even aware of my battle
Should I say something?
Do you want me to initiate?
Until the friction in my heart subsides
I remain taking the gasps for oxygen
Every so often
While I'm around you

Broken Cupboard

Every glass in the cupboard
Cracked and rusted
Shards of delicacy ready to draw the red river within it
And every time I get close
Thinking your pieces had been sanded down from our master craftsman
Your sharp edges stab my already ripe wounds you created

My long for nearness in the cabinet with you is running out
Kinship turned stone
Thoughts of you now vengeful fragments
Once beating with cherishment and love
But your lack of care and thoughtfulness
Has pierced too much of my heart
My spot
Vulnerable
I've lost too much blood

Little left to warm my deteriorated cup
Yet gentle hands take me out of the cupboard for repair
No, not bandaid patchwork
But His tender healing artistry
Takes the razor edges of my heart and runs the life water until smooth
surface is revealed again

In my absence
Dust
And maybe even a new piece of china
But I am more put together now
And my cup is called beloved

Disconnected Reality

Distractions in every sense of the word
All around us
And we give them such life
Polished smart gadgets that manufacture
our lethargic ways, and we like it
Plugging into our device and pulling the plug
with the existing surrounding us
Spending hours tuning out voices yet turning up
the many voices of comments on said photograph
Editing our lives to the superficial filter of perfection while
praying that no one sees through the refined smile
Counterfeit satisfaction accompanying the instantaneous
connection and warping our view of human response
Our lives slowly losing charge as soon as we pull away
from the life source of being present
And at our departure,
detaching from our virtual lives seems impossible
Because it is like our appendage
A part of us
Pursuing our advancement
Yet decreasing our humanity
Objective: Unity
Reality: Disconnection

My Apologies to You, Abuela

Your hands slaved away in the factory building for the Man
Beautiful accent a foreigner in this country
Got my lips from you and my hips from you
and I've never been thankful
Curvy girls were not "in" in my
predominantly white school growing up
I was too "ethnic" for the washboard blondies
And to think I was embarrassed because
your native tongue wasn't theirs
I did not know how blessed I was and am to have you
I was embarrassed for what you were shamed for your whole life
Your culture
Our family
Your touchy, sassy Puerto Rican spirit and my
do-anything-to-fit-in attitude
Wrecked my opportunity to invest
I'm sorry, abuela
You deserve to be celebrated and cherished
for you were a wise warrior

-ama a su nieta que se extraña

Captain's Foreigner

You are the Captain of my thoughts
Your demeanor I see on strangers,
hoping that you have returned
Thousands of miles between us
& part of me wishes my heart wasn't an alien
Your lure in me is deep and has left me with an infinity of what if's

A piece of me wishes that parting letter was a confession
instead of the ode to our friendship
But I couldn't bring myself to the thought
of losing anything with you

And now I don't want the thoughts to cease,
your ship to finally set sail
Dreaming of futures with your face beside mine is safe
But you have no idea
Of me
Of my what ifs

The Florida sun hasn't seen you for months now
And I have become jealous of the Pittsburgh air

And that's how it'll stay
My dreaming
You living
Foreigners to each other's hearts

Divided

The downpour of crummy-afternoon into wet vans
Where the warm, polished sand seems to live too

A utopia of infinite Benjamin-pocketed men
Bleached bikini women with false lips like Barbie herself

While across the bridge
The land of mini dinosaurs, sweaty-dirty laundry and
Sidewalks full of hungry panhandlers

The scope is roomy enough it's sickening

The natives sharing their room with hundreds of reptile hearts
Yet across the water
The empty mansions creak with loneliness
for the birds are still up north

What are we really doing in this divided city?

Toes

Whore Toes.

selling themselves to the grounds of here and there
gaining miles in pursuit of a cause
frequently with different beholders

some painted periwinkle with a glossy smile, showing no lack of up-keep
some painted with chips of character missing and life-lived
some naked and raw for the world to see and know

toes with the daily cotton suffocating mask
shoved and crammed every morning in the same old leather bound life
the bearers of different sizes and different colors

the grime aims to define them as used and dirty
but no toes are too filthy for His washcloth
for any amount of dirt, stench, wounds, or mistakes
nothing
can be considered "too messy" for the ultimate Cleanser

yes, whore toes get around
walk in wrong directions
dip themselves into uncertain waters
Some of which have a sting, a burn
leaving scars
though, properly tended to, toes can heal
washed of the waters they've been through
they can be made beautiful
whore toes and all

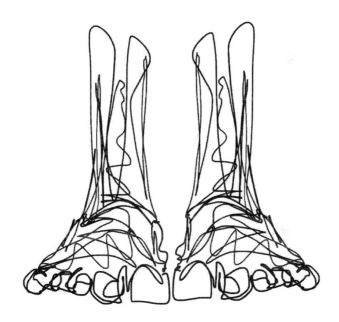

Melancholy Debate

Because I have a disposition towards the melancholy
The agony and heartbreak is so familiar I crave it
Trauma has caused me to miss the addiction of abuse
To stew in my tears and victimhood
Is to give into the narrative that I am and will always be that girl
For as much as I yearn not to be
In the friendly pit of hopelessness lies a gravestone
with my full name engraved
To overcome the pervasive sadness is to suggest that all its
presence never was
The impact that it has had
Meaningless
Which I dare not do
Ignorance of the past wounds doesn't allow me to claim freedom
But neither does holding back healing from my decades-deep
flesh wounds
Still I breathe in and out the same air
Mine still just tasting unbearably thick
rather than free and joyfully light

Join Me on the Blanket

I tell all my secrets to the ocean
It is my constant until you take its place
The sand is where I sit in patience
It holds me until you are ready to
Vulnerable
The wind tells me the powerful feelings
that I long to hear from your lips instead
I experience every sunrise love story
And eagerly wait to write one with you
Beautiful
Unique
Undeniably ours
But don't worry
I'll sit here until you join me on the blanket
I'm trying to be as patient as I can be
Don't wait too long, hun
The sand gets jealous of the space reserved for you

My Villains

Isolation is the villain of my night
Him and his friend loneliness
They don't hold back
and never give notice of their surprised entrance
Like a reunion party that I was never invited to
A group of intruders in my home
They creep in and tear down the sweet-souled Joy that abides
They tell her she isn't permanent and remind her
that she's unworthy of the body she inhabits

They make their nest while slowly killing their host
I try to fight but my strength is the size of an apple seed
in the pit of my stomach

Damn you isolation
You are the lie from the enemy who attempts to rip me from
the goodness and abundance of my eternal
You make me feel like I'm on an island of crazies
where I'm the president and the population is one

& Damn you loneliness
You make me feel unworthy of any love and like a leper that has
been exiled
For you haunt my past, present, and future thoughts
You are my biggest terror

And enough is enough

Code

Centuries old, invisible stone tablets of loyalty
Women's blood shared with the closest of friends
These promises deem their souls royalty
And the men fall peasant and slave
Queens in their kingdoms with sisters,
unbreakable as Palomar knots
To whom a Queen's heart favors becomes the blacklist
of chosen lovers for her sisters
This blacklist mirrors the code
A queen that pursues a king, jester, or knight in another's land
has forever burned to ash her accord of the sorority
Let us remind our females
that this is the underlying summit of our commitment
The code must not be broken
For if it is she be cast out of the heart forever

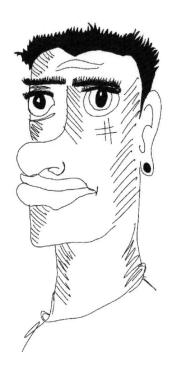

Walls

Built from pain and sorrow, your walls are constructed
Each stone manufactured letting no one see past it
The grand barricade of your concealed heart
Longs,
Longs to crumble like the walls of Jericho
Grain by grain I attempt to pull back your mighty stonework
Expectant to find another obstacle waiting for my conquer
You expect these walls to hold your safety
But at times your masonry lacking
For I am able to peek through your fractures
and see a gentle giant
And I will not waiver in my pursuit of you
No matter your blockades, or quest to keep yourself protected
Your soul is meant to be treasured and known
Your frail structure won't keep me out
What you don't realize is your defence is feeble
Together our stonework fused will better defend your enemies
You must let me in
I will continue to overthrow your walls
In search for your soul
Because every wall is worth the battle
For what lies within

Stopped at the Light

Your signs are as obvious as a green light
Yet your words scream yellow with caution
of almost no existence
I wonder
Am I making this up in my head
All the notes of your gaze
Your words
Your hands sliding down my back and for what
Just friendship
Please stop sitting afraid at the yellow light when I have been
waiting so anxious on the other side of the street
that could be named ours

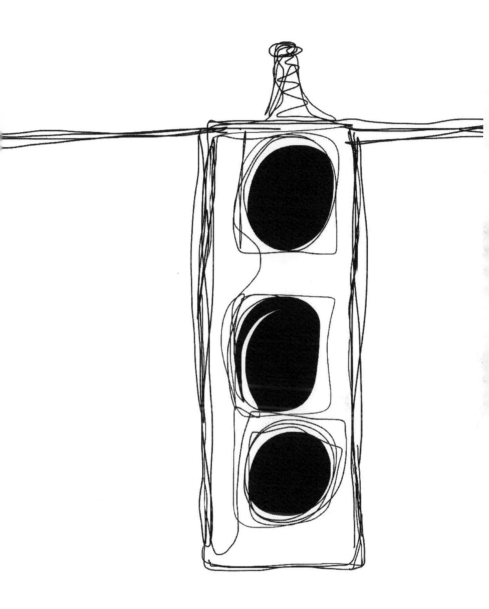

Breakups in December

Breakups in December suck
Like walking around with an open wound
While others are snuggling and sharing hot coco
The crisp air seems to fit the foreign silent nights that have begun
And now there is no one to say goodnight to and good morning

When I wake, I think about how no one will check in on me
I hurt inside trying to remember how this was normal before I met you
You changed me
Became a heart teacher
You became the evidence of what I had thought I already had known

Every time I think I have no tears left to give
Our song will come on
Or I see your photograph
Your favorite thing appears and all I can think about is laying in that
bed with you
watching all your favorite movies
I'm pulled in close
You playing with my hair
Every time putting me right to sleep 5 minutes into the movie

You have erased me from the newsfeed of the worlds insight
And that is what hurts the most
Now I am trying to erase the pixelated moments to cloud the
memories that we shared

My stomach has lost its appetite and is just hungry for a message
from you
I wanted you to fight for us
You so easily caved
No interest in the battle for a future us

And all I can think is
Breakups really do suck in December and well so do you

I Need Both

My heart is the strongest force of my being
My compass
Oh how the depths of that room make space for all the pain,
darkness, joy, and love
I crave more of my reason
For him to speak up
To show himself and be useful in my desires
My heart allows no face time for reason
For he thinks he does not act out of my best interest
But one who only listens to one
loses the perspective of clarity and reality
I beg you heart to share your space
Reason has the right
And please reason grow in confidence
I need you both like chaperones, leading my needy soul
And most of all
Reason and Heart be influenced by the Great Authority
Only then may this ship you are guiding find its way

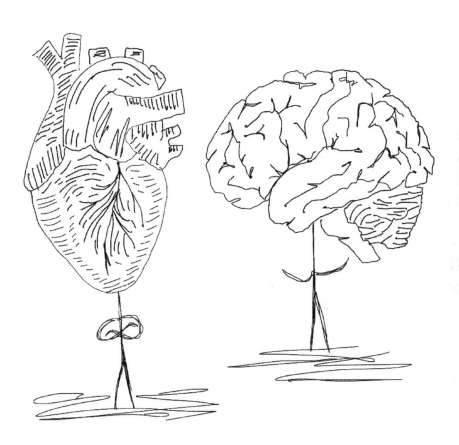

You Are Not Welcome

My skin you saw as candy to steal as you walked by and it seems
you're always hungry

Your filthy palms claiming what was never theirs, declaring ownership,
while making my own home feel like I'm the visitor

And as I feel your grip my breath is lost
Words locked so tightly unable to form two letters together into anything
All of me sunken into a pit as the throne of my temple is being invaded

My hands as your controller playing only the game you want
Your fingers seizing my neck keeping me close
And that's where it starts
Your game and your feast
An attendance of one

And I thought it wouldn't happen again
Not with the better friends I had around me now
The 180 change was for the better
So how am I here again?
The object instead of human
My body parts as your appetizers
Your harsh grasp withstanding my resistance
And there I end up
Motionless waiting for you to finish your robbery
So I lay waiting to recover once more

To start the healing process of learning my sanctuary is mine
and no one else's

The confidence that an "n" and an "o" can be spoken again
Understanding that others will view this as my fault
That I put myself there
Even though they don't understand
That I never wanted it
I never asked for it
That he wanted it
And never asked for it
Because he just assumed
Like they always do

Your invasion is over
Your grip on me is finished
The reign you once had, destroyed
This body is too precious to settle for a ravenous trespasser
that doesn't value the native

Take your manipulative stomach somewhere else because you
will not be satisfied here anymore

Risk

A risk?
I am
Healing has come here
Restoration, my anthem cry
Though shattered and broken in your eyes
The pit in my stomach from the poisoned lie that I am not worthy

But you are not the one who decides
A title
An opinion
Doesn't take that from me
So sure, I'm a risk
Because love is the risk
If no one took a chance on me, the growth I wouldn't have seen

-     the one you missed out on

Powerless

Losing sight of each passing ship of opportunity
Waiting
Wanting that thing called control
To anchor a life of picture perfect quality in our hand
to show others
And it always seems either just over the horizon or worlds away
The distance enough to be just out of our grasp
And we are eternally left with this dilemma
No way to finesse life to the way we want
Leaving us seemingly, and always,
Powerless

Soul on Wholesale

Angry I sit
Unable to control the switch of my emotions
From silent benevolence I drink the love potion
That is killing me inside

You aren't aware of my heart strings
Fastened to your longing eyes and lip lickings
I hang on to every gaze towards mine
Praying you'll catch on

And you don't
Still haven't

So my unmet expectations
Leave me with complete concentration
Of your every breath
Movement
and
Words

Towards me or any other female
Jealousy feels like my soul is on wholesale
But please
Continue to tell me about your ex girlfriend
And how the relationship is one you hope to mend

It helps

Me get over you
You clueless
Dumb
Boy
I'm beginning to hate you

Homesick

I am left with a gaping wound
The feeling of insufficiency tattooed on my forehead
Yet, you tell me I have nothing to prove
Because you have "done it all"

But my heart drips blood with the lack of affection
Yearning to taste you
To feel complete
And I miss your intimacy
The familiarity of the world's dissatisfying water hurts
But at least I felt something

Oh God, I am homesick
How I wish you'd come

And the thing is, you have
My heart has not been aware of you
But the footprints of my lacking are traced with your nearness
The clouded vision of my eyes leaves me lost
And I wonder when you will finally show your face

Anxiety

I cannibalize my thought process
An unrecoverable thought tornado
My insides shaking like an earthquake beneath my heart
I
can't
breathe
All the thoughts
Their voices so loud that
The constant noise makes the world around me
feel like it's spinning
Reaching two fingers pressed to my warm neck to
check my own pulse
Such an out of body experience
I need to make sure it's still there
Help

I
can't
just
breathe
and choose to stop thinking about what I can't control
It's harder than those words that I easily want to believe
That command
STOP
I'm trying

I'm trying

Keep trying

Missing Heart

Once dreamt of our lips touching and bodies pressed
up against each other
And the night finally happened
You embraced me
Held me tight
Danced on the beach with me under the stars
Held my hand close
Kissed me and I met your tongue that knew it's way around mine
For hours we seemed to be in the movie I begged you
to watch with me for years

But I felt nothing
Nothing towards you
The intimacy that I had craved, barely even quenched
No emotions needed, really

In a sense, I am relieved
For my own heart to not be loving yours anymore

But also worried that I will never feel what love is truly like

The one guy I thought I actually loved in this world
and nothing
No romantic butterflies
No holding my breath

Worried that my heart line has become disconnected
Cut off
From the normal headquarters of my soul

SOS
Lost heart?
If anyone finds her
Please send her home in one piece

My Psalm

For you are slow to anger
Even with the fallen
Your boundless grace
Your ceaseless love
Is never withheld
While the commoner's heart is out to seek vengeance
Your heart is out to show them affection

Sad Truth

For as much as I try
I hurt others
The condition of humanity involves pain
People are like a messy bag of leftovers
The blend of diverse realities will inevitably cause discomfort
We are harsh with language
We inflict suffering to others' hearts
I hurt others
And am not the best lover out there
But neither are you

Cycle

My days go like this:

I'm single and I hate it

I'm single and I love it

Long for Aslan

I cry out for a lion heart
One with a strong foundation
To combat the shame-filled judgments cast into my space
Bring healing into my trauma-wired thoughts
Repurpose my temple for your goodness
Fill the desert valleys with your living stream
For heaven's sake
Allow my mind to be yours and end the survival tactics I use
Guide me in the search for a courageous yet God-fearing heart
As brave and fierce as wildcat
And as empathetic and faithful as Aslan himself

My Hope for Us

We met in a moment with no expectation
Not knowing my heart would soon be consumed with a new motivation

Of knowing you
Being with you
My prayers involving you

And I feel crazy because the of speed of our soul connection
But I sit excited to see where all of this, you & me will take direction

Towards affection
With the protection
Of our heavenly father's correction
Of the way we care for each other through our imperfections

So as I pause and pray for us
To keep our God in the center is a must

So my dear, all I can do is ask
For you to live without a mask

Run to the father first
And sit and listen
Our growth & health should be our mission

Our hearts will grow together
When we love God and love people better

Deep and wide from our Source
You are who I want to do this thing with of course

My War

Every morning when the sun kisses the earth good morning
And my feet hit the ground
The battle begins
The invisible war in my mind
As it hosts the never ending sucker punches loneliness gives
The false narratives that I will never been enough
Or worthy of pursuit strike my chest before I can lift my fist to
block them

By the end of the day, knuckles bleeding
Body aching from the fight
I question why I didn't put my armour on this morning
My armour of protection
The weapons that have been written on my heart to use in the fight
The source of my great Ally who has already claimed victory on
my day of challenges and the battles for all my tomorrows

Oh dear Father
Help me understand and declare triumph in your name
Shield me
Cover my hands with the confidence of your promises
Give my body protection from the stories of hurt that have be-
come the air to my lungs, toxic
Remind me to place my feet in the peace of your gospel
Allow my heart to continue to petition for your strength
and not my own

I do not stand a chance against the blows to my heart the enemy
executes
He is built of stealth
Oh Omniscient Savior
Liberate my mind and heart to dwell on
the ease of You in this war

Thank you for being a great friend and reading pieces of my heart.

This book is an invitation to a conversation. A conversation about the process and the Ultimate Healer who has aided me most in this process. I personally invited you into my process, and this is an open door to talk about ours.

We were made for fullness and entering into the process of understanding our story and how it shapes us is just the beginning.

May you find healing, growth and confidence in sharing your process with others.

Congratulations and welcome
to **The Society of Process.**

-Hailey Paige

ABOUT THE AUTHOR

Hailey Paige is the author and illustrator behind **The Society of Process**. She grew up in a blended family in northeast Ohio but currently resides in West Palm Beach, Florida. Hailey is currently pursuing her masters degree in clinical mental health with a concentration in trauma and crisis counseling from Palm Beach Atlantic University. She is also a teacher and specializes in social immersion with students with prolific behavioral needs, many of whom are on the autism spectrum. This work and specific demographic has become a passion of hers. Hailey loves to travel, connect with strangers, and create art along the way. As a student of and advocate for mental health, she is committed to the process of helping others in their healing and growth, as she continues to lean into hers.

.

Made in the USA
Columbia, SC
13 March 2020